In Progress

Road to PhD

PhD in Progress

Vector Images from www.freepik.com

Congratulations!

Your PhD is in progress....
Let's continue your journey...
Set your goals here....

PhD is possible at any age! Do your best.......

MY PROFILE

Name : ______________________________

Sponsor : ______________________________

Matric No. : ______________________________

Institution : ______________________________

Email : ______________________________

Details of Programme

Programme of Study	☐ PhD ☐ Master	
Field of Specialization	☐ Electrical ☐ ____________ ☐ Manufacturing ☐ ____________ ☐ ICT ☐ ____________	
Type of Registration	☐ Full Time ☐ Part Time	
Semester	*First Registration*	*Expected Completion of Studies*
Name of Supervisor(s)	1. ____________________ 2. ____________________ 3. ____________________	

The Three Elements of Research Title

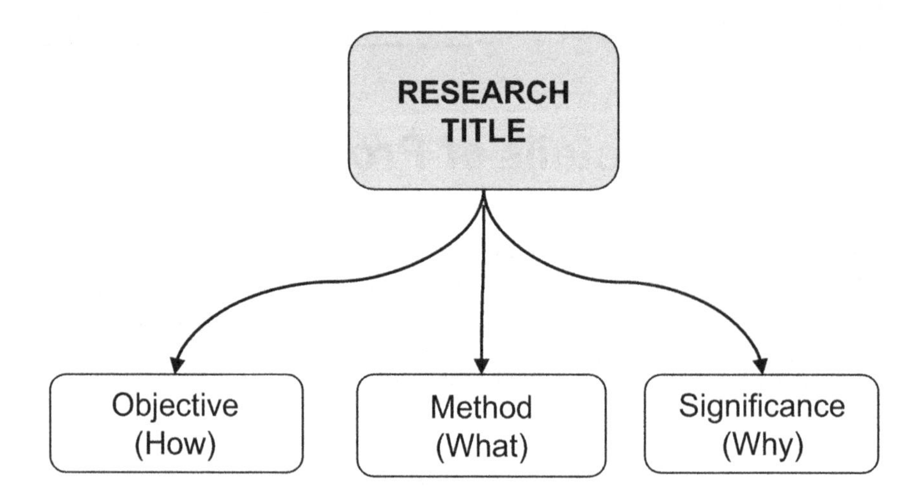

Research Title

Has three main important components; **Objective, Method,** and **Significance.** List all the suggestion titles here and select the best title for your research.

Your Research Title

01 ______________________________ ☐

____

02 ______________________________ ☐

____

03 ______________________________ ☐

____

04 ______________________________ ☐

____

05 ______________________________ ☐

____

06 ______________________________ ☐

____

Starting a PhD

How to Start?

Set Goals

Make a Progress

Be Visible

Understand the Background

Find the Gaps

Design Solution

Validate and Evaluate

Write and Publish

Share and Connect

SET YOUR TIMELINE!

Best wishes with all your plans...

YEAR (_____)

Research Activities

Q1 (Jan – Mac)	Q2 (Apr - Jun)

01

Research Activities

Q3 (Jul - Sept)	Q4 (Oct - Dec)

YEAR (_____)

Research Activities

Q1 (Jan – Mac)	Q2 (Apr - Jun)

02

Research Activities	Q3 (Jul - Sept)	Q4 (Oct - Dec)

YEAR (______)

Research Activities	Q1 (Jan – Mac)	Q2 (Apr - Jun)

03

Research Activities	Q3 (Jul - Sept)	Q4 (Oct - Dec)

YEAR (_____)

Research Activities

Q1 (Jan – Mac)	Q2 (Apr - Jun)

Research Activities

Q3 (Jul - Sept)	Q4 (Oct - Dec)

YEAR (_____)

Research Activities

Q1 (Jan – Mac)	Q2 (Apr - Jun)

05

Research Activities	Q3 (Jul - Sept)	Q4 (Oct - Dec)

To-do List

List all the research activities here:

No.	Task	Status

To-do List

List all the research activities here:

No.	Task	Status

MONTHLY PLAN

MONTH:

MONTHLY GOALS:

MON	TUE	WED	THU	FRI	SAT	SUN

NOTE

MONTHLY PLAN

MONTHLY GOALS:

MONTH:

MON	TUE	WED	THU	FRI	SAT	SUN

NOTE

MONTHLY PLAN

MONTHLY GOALS:

MONTH:

MON	TUE	WED	THU	FRI	SAT	SUN

NOTE

MONTHLY PLAN

MONTH:

MONTHLY GOALS:

MON	TUE	WED	THU	FRI	SAT	SUN

NOTE

MONTHLY PLAN

MONTHLY GOALS:

MONTH:

MON	TUE	WED	THU	FRI	SAT	SUN

NOTE

MONTHLY PLAN

MONTH:

MONTHLY GOALS:

MON	TUE	WED	THU	FRI	SAT	SUN

NOTE

MONTHLY PLAN

MONTHLY GOALS:

MONTH:

MON	TUE	WED	THU	FRI	SAT	SUN

NOTE

MONTHLY PLAN

MONTH:

MONTHLY GOALS:

MON	TUE	WED	THU	FRI	SAT	SUN

NOTE

MONTHLY PLAN

MONTH:

MONTHLY GOALS:

MON	TUE	WED	THU	FRI	SAT	SUN

NOTE

MONTHLY PLAN

MONTHLY GOALS:

MONTH:

MON	TUE	WED	THU	FRI	SAT	SUN

NOTE

MONTHLY PLAN

MONTH:

MONTHLY GOALS:

MON	TUE	WED	THU	FRI	SAT	SUN

NOTE

MONTHLY PLAN

MONTH:

MONTHLY GOALS:

MON	TUE	WED	THU	FRI	SAT	SUN

NOTE

"A Journey of A Thousand Miles Must Begin with A Single Step"

~ Lao Tzu

PROGRESS OF STUDIES

(Chapter completed and progress to date)

Session/ Year						
Number of Planned Chapters						
Number of Completed Chapters						
Percentage of Progress (%)						
Expected Date/New Date of Thesis Draft Submission						

Data Collection

(Tick where appropriate)

1	2	3	4	5	6	7	8	9	10

Start **Complete**

Data Analysis

(Tick where appropriate)

1	2	3	4	5	6	7	8	9	10

Start Complete

PROGRESS
LOG BOOK

To-do List

List all the research activities here:

No.	Task	Due Date	Status

To-do List

List all the research activities here:

No.	Task	Due Date	Status

My Progress

Date:

Task	Status	Actions

Important Things:

Date:

My Progress

Task	Status	Actions

Important Things:

My Progress

Date:

Task	Status	Actions

Important Things:

Date:

My Progress

Task	Status	Actions

Important Things:

My Progress

Date:

Task	Status	Actions

Important Things:

My Progress

Date:

Task	Status	Actions

Important Things:

Date:

My Progress

Task	Status	Actions

Important Things:

My Progress

Date:

Task	Status	Actions

Important Things:

MY ACHIEVEMENTS!

List of paper published/ presented, seminar attended, etc.

Journal

No.	Research Title/ Journal/ Volume/ Year	Fee	Index

Journal

No.	Research Title/ Journal/ Volume/ Year	Fee	Index

Proceeding

No.	Research Title/ Proceeding/ Volume/ Year	Venue/ Fee	Index

Proceeding

No.	Research Title/ Proceeding/ Volume/ Year	Venue/ Fee	Index

Book Chapter

No.	Research Title/ Book Chapter	Publisher	Index

Non-Academic Activities

No.	Activities	Status

Non-Academic Activities

No.	Activities	Status

RESEARCH SOFTWARE

Grammarly

Grammar Check

QuillBot | REF-N-WRITE

Paraphrasing Tool

Turnitin

Plagiarism Checker

NVIVO | ATLAS.ti

Qualitative Data Analysis

SPSS

Quantitative Data Analysis

Mendeley

EndNote

Scholarcy

Reference Management

PLS-SEM

Multivariate Analysis

Research Tools

My favourite research tools are…

01 ______________________________

____

02 ______________________________

____

03 ______________________________

____

04 ______________________________

____

05 ______________________________

____

06 ______________________________

____

07 ______________________________

____

08 ______________________________

____

Research Tools

My favourite research tools are…

01 ______________________________

02 ______________________________

03 ______________________________

04 ______________________________

05 ______________________________

06 ______________________________

07 ______________________________

08 ______________________________

Research Tools

My favourite research tools are…

01

02

03

04

05

06

07

08

WORKSHOP NOTES

Workshop : ______________________________

Date : ______________________________

Speaker : ______________________________

Venue : ______________________________

Fee : ______________________________

Notes:

Draw a mind map:

Workshop : ______________________________

Date : ______________________________

Speaker : ______________________________

Venue : ______________________________

Fee : ______________________________

Notes:

Draw a mind map:

Workshop : ______________________________

Date : ______________________________

Speaker : ______________________________

Venue : ______________________________

Fee : ______________________________

Notes:

Draw a mind map:

Workshop : ______________________________

Date : ______________________________

Speaker : ______________________________

Venue : ______________________________

Fee : ______________________________

Notes:

Draw a mind map:

Workshop : ______________________________

Date : ______________________________

Speaker : ______________________________

Venue : ______________________________

Fee : ______________________________

Notes:

Draw a mind map:

BE VISIBLE!

Enhance visibility and impact.
Make sure to build your network.

Research Gate

LinkedIn

Academia

Publon

Google Scholar

Promote your publication to get more citations.

“Wake Up Every Morning With The Thought That Something Wonderful Is About To Happen”

~ Anonymous

RESEARCH PROCESS

Flow Chart of a Research Process

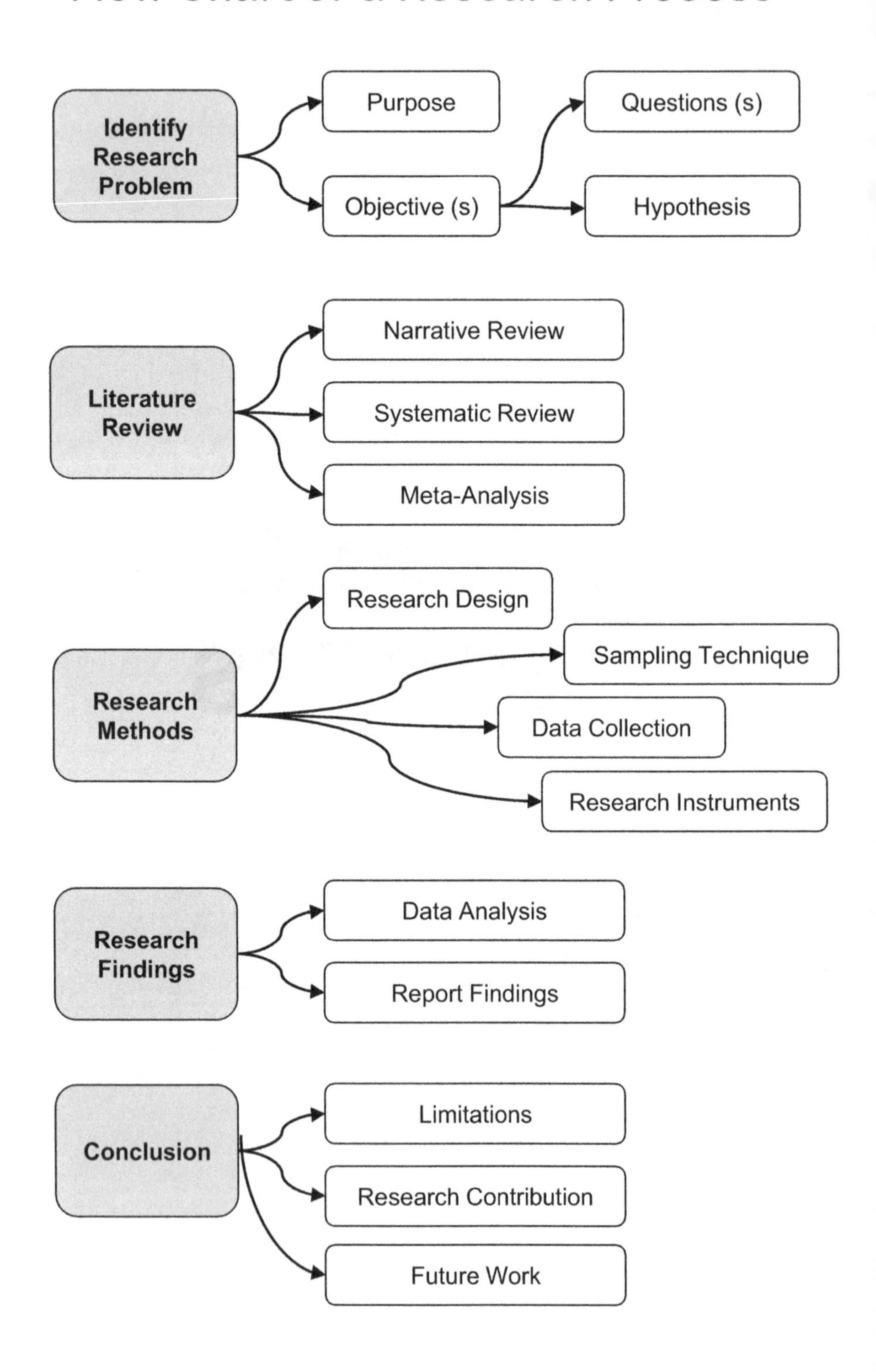

01

Identify Research Problem

The research problem is the heart of a study. To begin, you will need to know where to look for your research problems.

PROBLEM STATEMENTS

Problem Statements

No.	Research Gaps/ Current Issues	References

Problem Statements

No.	Research Gaps/ Current Issues	References

Problem Statements

No.	Research Gaps/ Current Issues	References

RESEARCH OBJECTIVES

Tips:

Examples of research objectives:

To check whether there is a relationship between....

To investigate existing .....

To determine factor that enhances ....

To design tools for ....

To perform a meta-analysis of .....

To propose a new model .....

To propose a new approach ....

To construct a new framework .....

To formulate a new algorithm .....

To evaluate the effectiveness of ......

To validate the proposed model .....

Make sure that the Research Question (RQ) and Research Objective (RO) are **answerable, feasible** and **relevant.**

Develop a Research Hypothesis (RH) from the RQ.

S.M.A.R.T

Specific | Measurable |Achievable | Relevant | Time-bound

Research Objectives

01 ______________________________

____

02 ______________________________

____

03 ______________________________

____

04 ______________________________

____

05 ______________________________

____

Use action verbs to write your objectives:

- To identify
- To determine
- To analyse
- To investigate
- To understand
- To propose
- To construct
- To design
- To develop
- To generate
- To compare
- To test
- To validate
- To integrate
- To classify

Research Summaries

No	Research Gaps/ Current Issues	Research Objective (RO)

Research Summaries

No	Research Question (RQ)	Research Hypothesis (RH)

DEFINITION OF TERMS

Definition of Terms

Term	Description

Definition of Terms

Term	Description

Definition of Terms

Term	Description

RESEARCH APPROACH

Research Approaches

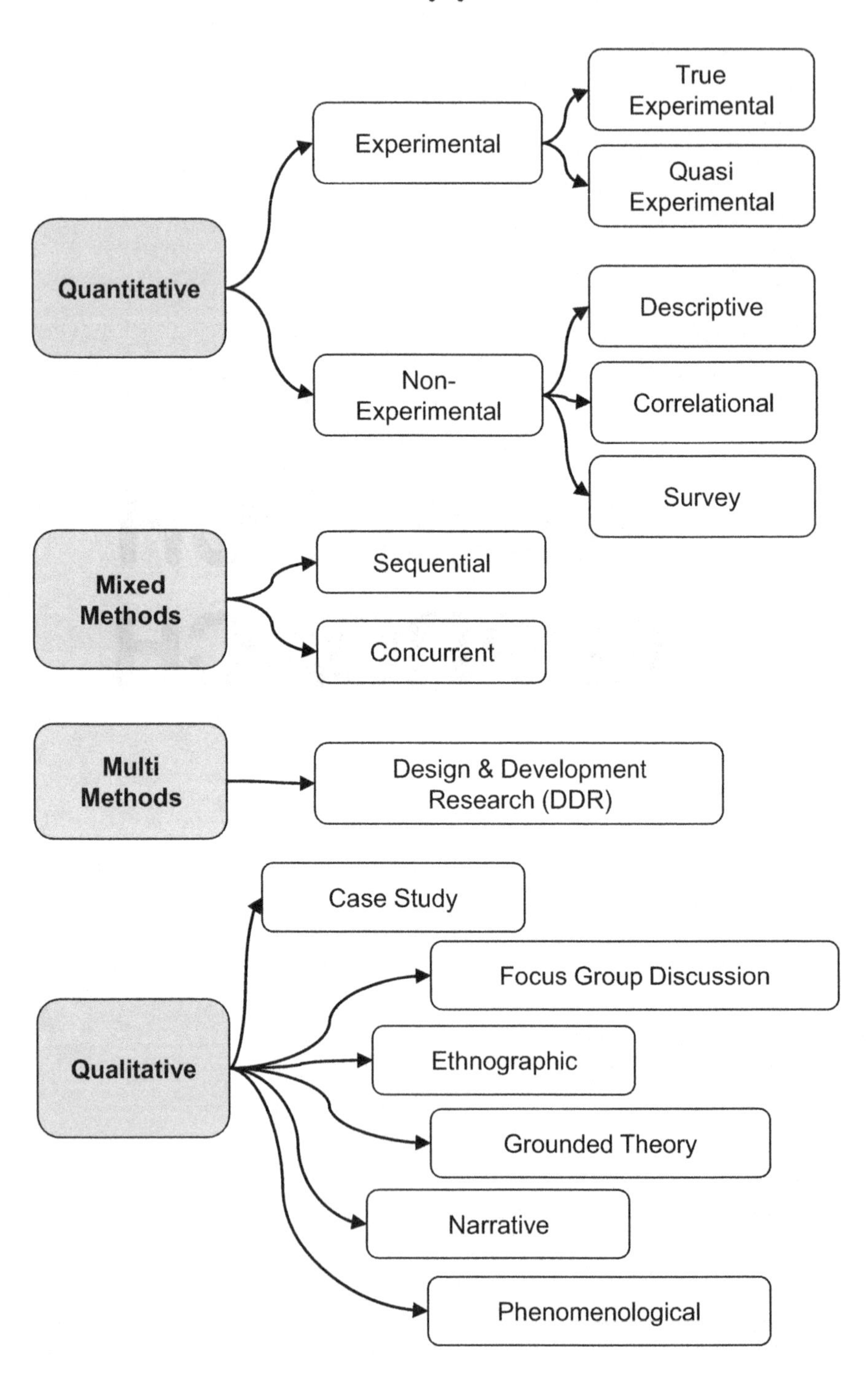

02

Literature Review

Types of Literature

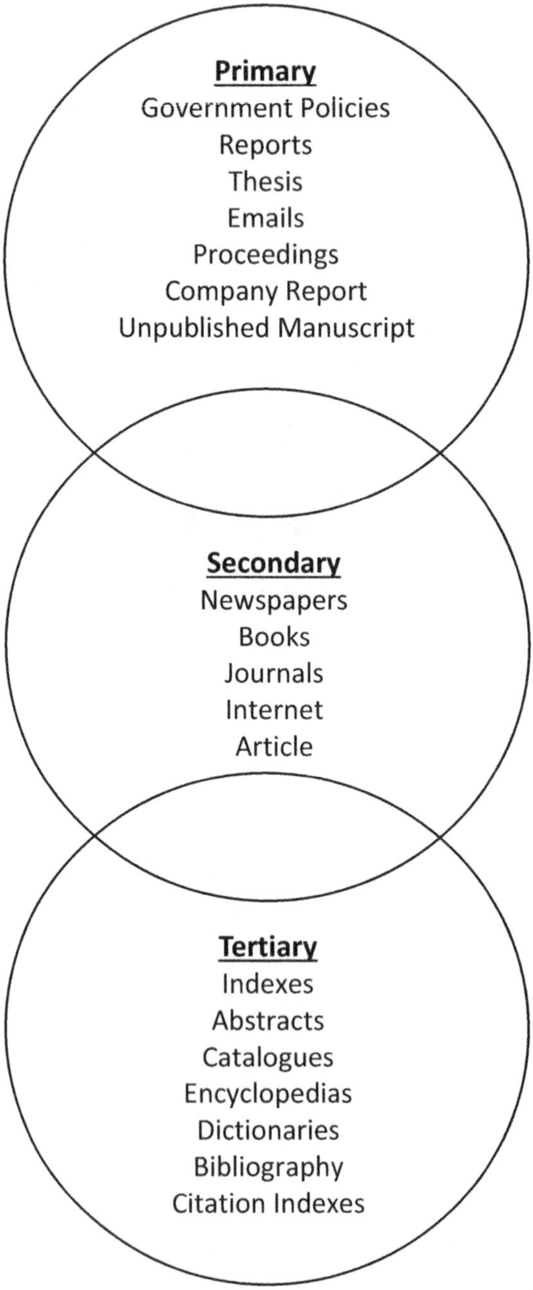

Primary
Government Policies
Reports
Thesis
Emails
Proceedings
Company Report
Unpublished Manuscript

Secondary
Newspapers
Books
Journals
Internet
Article

Tertiary
Indexes
Abstracts
Catalogues
Encyclopedias
Dictionaries
Bibliography
Citation Indexes

SEARCHING THE LITERATURE

Web of Science

Scopus

Springer

Research Gate

Science Hub

Academia

Elsevier

Google Scholar

Science Direct

Research Tools

My favourite research tools are…

01 ______________________________

____

02 ______________________________

____

03 ______________________________

____

04 ______________________________

____

05 ______________________________

____

06 ______________________________

____

07 ______________________________

____

08 ______________________________

____

Research Tools

My favourite research tools are…

01 ______________________________

____

02 ______________________________

____

03 ______________________________

____

04 ______________________________

____

05 ______________________________

____

06 ______________________________

____

07 ______________________________

____

08 ______________________________

____

Steps of Literature Review

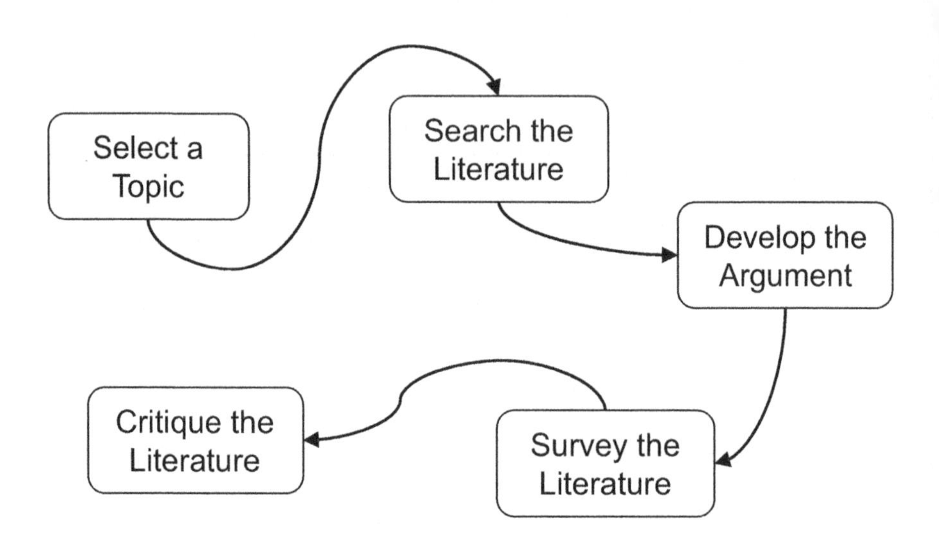

Notes:

- Read as much as possible to increase knowledge and familiarity with the topic and to assist with research development.
- Learn about the current trends and technological advances on the topic. Take note of the different trends in the literature.

READ JOURNALS

Title	
Authors	
Journal	
Vol./ No./ Year	

Title	
Authors	
Journal	
Vol./ No./ Year	

Title	
Authors	
Journal	
Vol./ No./ Year	

Title	
Authors	
Journal	
Vol./ No./ Year	

Title	
Authors	
Journal	
Vol./ No./ Year	

Title	
Authors	
Journal	
Vol./ No./ Year	

Summaries of Literature Study

References	RO/ RQ/ RH	Methods

Summaries of Literature Study

Findings	Research Gaps	Limitation

Summaries of Literature Study

References	RO/ RQ/ RH	Methods

Summaries of Literature Study

Findings	Research Gaps	Limitation

Summaries of Literature Study

References	RO/ RQ/ RH	Methods

Summaries of Literature Study

Findings	Research Gaps	Limitation

Summaries of Literature Study

References	RO/ RQ/ RH	Methods

Summaries of Literature Study

Findings	Research Gaps	Limitation

03

Research Methods

Research Design

Quantitative | Mixed Methods | Multi Methods | Qualitative

Ethical Matters

Sampling Technique

Random Sampling | Purposeful Ransom Sampling | Convenience Sampling | Stratified Sampling | Criterion Sampling | Snowball Sampling | Homogenous Sampling

Research Instruments

Survey | Interview | Observation | Pre-Test | Post-test

Likert-Type Scale Response Anchors

Citation:
Vagias, Wade M. (2006). *Likert-type Scale Response Anchors*. Clemson International Institute for Tourism & Research Development, Department of Parks, Recreation and Tourism Management. Clemson University.

Level of Agreement
1 – Strongly disagree
2 – Disagree
3 – Neither agree or disagree
4 – Agree
5 – Strongly agree

Level of Agreement
1 – Strongly disagree
2 – Disagree
3 – Somewhat disagree
4 – Neither agree or disagree
5 – Somewhat agree
6 – Agree
7 – Strongly agree

Level of Importance
1 – Not at all important
2 – Low importance
3 – Slightly important
4 – Neutral
5 – Moderately important
6 – Very important
7 – Extremely important

Priority Level
1 – Not a priority
2 – Low priority
3 – Medium priority
4 – High priority
5 – Essential

Frequency – 5 point
1 – Never
2 – Rarely
3 – Sometimes
4 – Often
5 – Always

Level of Problem
1 – Not at all a problem
2 – Minor problem
3 – Moderate problem
4 – Serious problem

Level of Participation
1 – No, and not considered
2 – No, but considered
3 – Yes

Level of Consideration
1 – Would not consider
2 – Might or might not consider
3 – Definitely consider

Likert-Type Scale Response Anchors

Amount of Use
1 – Never use
2 – Almost never
3 – Occasionally/Sometimes
4 – Almost every time
5 – Frequently use

Level of Satisfaction
1 – Very dissatisfied
2 – dissatisfied
3 – unsure
4 – satisfied
5 – Very satisfied

Level of Familiarity
1 – not at all familiar
2 – Slightly familiar
3 – Somewhat familiar
4 – Moderately familiar
5 – Extremely familiar

Level of Quality
1 – Poor
2 – Fair
3 – Good
4 – Very good
5 – Excellent

Level of Awareness
1 – not at all aware
2 – Slightly aware
3 – Somewhat aware
4 – Moderately aware
5 – Extremely aware

Level of Influence
1 – not at all influential
2 – slightly influential
3 – somewhat influential
4 – very influential
5 – extremely influential

Level of Difficulty
1 – Very difficult
2 – Difficult
3 – Neutral
4 – Easy
5 – Very easy

Good / Bad
1 – Very negative
2 –
3 – Neutral
4 –
5 – Very positive

Barriers
1 – Not a barrier
2 – Somewhat of a barrier
3 – Moderate barrier
4 – Extreme barrier

Level of Responsibility
1 – Not at all responsible
2 – somewhat responsible
3 – mostly responsible
4 – completely responsible

Survey

Survey

Interview

Observation

Other

DEAL WITH EXPERT!

Don't Forget To Prepare These Documents:

Student Confirmation Letter

Data Collection Letter

The Letter of Ethics

Appointment Letter as Expert

Validation Form

List of Experts

No	Name, Institution, Email	Expertise	Contact Number

List of Experts

No	Name, Institution, Email	Expertise	Contact Number

List of Experts

No	Name, Institution, Email	Expertise	Contact Number

04

Research Findings

Preliminary Analysis

Experimental

Alpha Testing

Beta Testing

Pilot Test

05

Conclusion

Limitations

No	Current Issues	Status

Research Contributions

No	List of Contributions

Future Research

No	Future Works

RESEARCH PROPOSAL CHECKLIST

“Believe In Yourself And All That You Are. Know That There Is Something Inside You That Is Greater Than Any Obstacle”

~ Christian D. Larson

Research Proposal Checklist

		Done (√)
01	Cover	☐
02	Table of Contents	☐
03	Abstract	☐
04	List of Tables	☐
05	List of Figures	☐
06	List of Abbreviations	☐
07	Chapter 1: Introduction	☐
	Research Background	
	Problem Statement	
	Research Objective, Questions & Hypothesis	
	Scope of Study	
	Significance of The Research	
	Definition of Terms	
08	Chapter 2: Literature Review	☐
09	Chapter 3: Methodology	☐
	Research Approaches	
	Population & Sampling	
10	References	☐
11	Appendix	☐

CHECKLIST FOR THESIS SUBMISSION

Thesis Submission Checklist

		Done (√)
01	Front (Hard) Cover of Thesis	☐
02	Pre-title Page	☐
03	Title page	☐
04	Abstract	☐
05	Acknowledgement	☐
06	Approval	☐
07	Declaration	☐
08	Dedication	☐
09	List of Tables	☐
10	List of Figures	☐
11	List of Abbreviations	☐
12	List of Publications	☐
13	Table of Contents	☐
14	Main Text of Thesis	☐
15	References	☐
16	Appendix	☐

Believe in Yourself!

REFERENCES

Your References

Your References

Your References

Your References

Made in United States
Orlando, FL
12 December 2023